Alfred Hayes

The Vale of Arden, and Other Poems

Alfred Hayes

The Vale of Arden, and Other Poems

ISBN/EAN: 9783744770958

Printed in Europe, USA, Canada, Australia, Japan

Cover: Foto ©Thomas Meinert / pixelio.de

More available books at **www.hansebooks.com**

CONTENTS

Dedication

TO MY WIFE

Beloved wife,
For ever mine, not by the rash
Consuming kiss
Whose fierce flame turns to early ash,
But by the love that is
The sunshine of the tree of life ;

Thy love, that lent
Its morning breath to song, hath hushed
My manlier lute ;
As birds that pipe when dawn is flushed,
Or eve is wan, are mute
At noontide of their full content.

When love had birth,
My heart became a secret shell
    Where many an air
Moaned of the sea of love—Ah! well,
    Those songs, my sweet, will share
Our slumber in the sacred earth;

    And now that day
Is darkened by the hand of death,
    In warning raised,
And the dread angel threateneth,
    While love recoils amazed,
The hour wherein the soul grows gray;

    Again my heart
Is shaken into song; for so
    I need thy love
As blossoms need the light, and know
    This paradise will prove
A wilderness if thou depart.

Therefore I crave
With all my selfish strength that thou
May'st close mine eyes,
Not I, belovéd, thine; death's brow
Frowns not on him that dies,
But him that kneels beside the grave.

Nor could my loss
So harm thee, as thy loss would blight
My lonelier soul;—
But ah! thy tears!—'tis well that night
Obscures the shore, where roll
The waters each must singly cross.

Is love afraid
Of love's best friend? Is it to see
His picture wear
Its highest holiest light, that He
Who painted love so fair
Hath edged it with so deep a shade?

Thy beauty glows
The brighter for this cloud, fair flower
Suffused with light
Of love's own sun, whose gracious powei
Evil and good unite
To praise, as all men praise the rose.

Still would I woo
To win thee, though I have by rote
Thy sure consent;
For thou art mistress of each note
Of love's sweet instrument,
And art as free as thou art true.

I ask no life
Beyond this homely earth, so God
The boon bestow
Of autumn calm, and, ere the sod
Receive us, days of snow
For closer nestling, faithful wife.

But whether long
Or brief our transient honeymoon,
We'll share at last
One dwelling, where in love's high noon
Our dearest days were passed,
Not far from Avon's slumber-song.

TO NORMAN GALE

*(With that portion of "A Fellowship in Song" entitled
"From Midland Meadows.")*

FRIEND, whom I met in fruitful days
Rambling amid sequestered ways
        Of rustic song,
These flowers, in midland meadows grown
While yet I walked and mused alone,
Pleased to be laid beside thine own,
        To thee belong.

We both have worshipped the pure rest
Of Arden's gently sloping breast,
        With faith sincere ;

The simple breadth of view, that fills
Our famished souls, the voice that stills,
The comfort of the lowly hills,
  To both are dear.

Oft have we blest each woodland throat,
Have held our breath for some rare note
  In secret brake ;
Together watched the moon sail through
Mysterious seas of hoary blue,
Or stars mid billowy clouds pursue
  Her amber wake ;

Then, flushed with winter's honest kiss,
Have heard the yule-log snap and hiss,
  While songs, unsung
By souls that glowed apart before,
Leapt from our spirits' molten ore,
As from the fire's refulgent core
  Tongue leapt to tongue.

Age will abate the lyric flame,
The grave's dull tooth consume our name ;
          But hap what may,
Friend, we have captured fugitive
Fine joys, whose music will outlive
All the discordant world can give
          Or take away.

THE VALE OF ARDEN

HERE, in this maze of stifling streets,
Where heaven's own eye looks sick and spent,
Where day to day care's curse repeats,
And nature's priceless poesy
Is bartered for a glittering discontent,
    I would not choose to die.

But when with weary feet I turn,
Baffled, from truth's continual quest,
And hope's rich bow hath ceased to burn,
And, heard afar, the curfew-bell
Calleth my heart home to the quiet breast
    Of her I love so well—

Dear mother Earth—I fain would watch
The wisdom of thy gradual ways
From underneath some ancient thatch,
Where all that toucheth eye or ear
Keepeth the simple tone of those good days
        When childhood's fount ran clear;

There to abide, and hold awhile
Communion with thy soul, and mark
Thy reverend visage frown and smile,
And woo the secret of the breeze,
While dawn grows noon and noon declines to dark
        By unperceived degrees;

So, made at one with thee, to taste
Contentment's temperate cup, nor spill
One precious drop in needless haste,
But, with youth's fever-dream subdued,
Let Nature's sovereign alchemy distil
        The balm of quietude;

B

And feel her healing influence fall,
As when upon a sufferer's head
A hand is laid, medicinal
To put the lean and clamorous brood
Of pain-begotten cares to flight, and spread
A slumber through the blood.

Embosomed shall my cottage be
In woodlands, whence the village spire
Peeps, and the overflowing glee
Of lips that cannot long be sad
Makes with the songbirds' sweet untutored quire
Music divinely glad ;

Not where the cloud-encumbered brows
Of mountains brood o'er barren dales,
And many a fretful torrent flows ;
Nor where, with slow-returning sigh,
The sleepless surge eternally bewails
Life's lonely mystery ;

But where, by moss-grown watermills
And willowy meadows fringed with reed,
Old Avon creeps beside the hills
That shelter, not seclude, the plain,
And peaceful kine o'er sunny pastures feed
    Refreshed with genial rain.

There, in the softly sloping lap
Of England's peace, where hedges trim
Chequer the lea, and mists enwrap
Each hidden hamlet, waits my home—
A drowsy region, friendly unto him
    That asks no more to roam;

There Shakespeare's self was moulded; there
He wooed his love, he wove his verse;
There his full soul grew ripe; and ere
His song was stilled, on that kind breast
Contented well to sleep, he laid a curse
    On who should break his rest.

A land where venerable trees
Whisper to many a storied grange,
Where orchards slumber, and the breeze
Comes laden with the breath of flowers,
And all things bask, and nothing swift or strange
Disturbs the loitering hours.

No sea-blast warps the stateliness
Of those great elms ; but wafted mild
From the warm hills the large airs bless
The mellow midland vale ; and all
That liveth where its generous sun hath smiled
Doth goodly grow and tall.

Not desolate is he that dwells
In that still country ; all around
Breathes a familiar voice, that tells
The soul's desire is satisfied,
And man with every earth-born thing is bound
In kindred close and wide.

The murmur of the haunted woods,
The sombre music of the storm,
The spell that o'er the distance broods,
In one broad harmony unite
Of peace, as blend the rainbow's tones to form
    The perfect chord of light;

And as of yore rich incense rose,
When on their knees the people fell
'Neath some vast dome, so all that grows
Beneath heaven's roof pays to the sun
Due worship of earth's sweet and wholesome smell,
    Mingling all life in one;

The fragrance of the fresh-turned loam,
Of hawthorn bloom and breathing hay,
The slumbrous air of harvest-home,
Find each in man their counterpart,
And make the echoes of old memories play
    About his listening heart;

Whether through greenwood shades he steals,
Or museth where the landscape sweeps
Into the realm of dream, he feels
A sense of great companionship,
Of one that knoweth all but ever keeps
A finger on the lip;

He hears—when not a blade is stirred,
And, muffled in dense foliage,
Only the call of some shy bird
Deepens the silence of the whole—
He hears a voice whose comfort can assuage
The fever of his soul.

Gently the seasons twine their arms,
Lingering amid those tranquil glades,
Relieving each the other's charms,
Waking and lulling pure desires—
A restful loveliness that never fades,
A change that never tires.

Spring trills her blithest carol there,
When cowslips fleck the glistening green,
When swallows cleave the gladsome air
With rapturous cries, and bursting buds
Breathe, after showers, a soft mysterious sheen
Along the sunlit woods.

There, when the hidden dove all day
Purrs in the coppice dim with heat,
Reclined beneath a wild-rose spray
June sleepeth in the still noontide,
While over fragrant fields of bean and wheat
The slow cloud-shadows glide.

But chiefly autumn loves to shed
Her placid sunshine o'er the vale,
When wide across the mead is spread
Warm river-mist, and the mild year
Dreameth, and orchards rich with fruit exhale
A lustrous atmosphere ;

Then sweet it is, with meek-eyed dawn,
While yet the shadows of the sheaves
Stretch far and faint, to pace the lawn
Dew-silvered; or to stray with her
By ragged hedgerows while the reddening leaves
    Are gray with gossamer;

To watch, when golden afternoon
Floodeth the garden's sanctuary,
Bees harvesting the blossom's boon,
Where mid the stately hollyhocks
Teems the rich hive, and flits the butterfly
    O'er flower-beds edged with box.

When winter's loud-lunged herald wears
His motley suit, 'tis good to mark
Storm-pennons, which the south wind tears
To tatters, stream across the sky,
And sun-gleams chequer hamlet, holt and park
    With wild emblazonry,

Chasing the shadows as they sweep
O'er stubble fields and withered sedge,
Gilding awhile the ricks that peep,
Fresh-thatched, where brooding yews protect
Some low-browed homestead on the river's edge,
Time-stained and ivy-decked.

Dear too are winter's sober skies
To him who pants for quiet ; all
The lavish autumn splendour lies
Asleep beneath its coverlet
Of fallen foliage ; and a purple pall
Clings, when the sun hath set,

To naked woods as soft as clouds ;
While with cold arm the saintly moon
Hallows the silent mist that shrouds
The darkening furrows, and a calm
Unfelt in springtime's morn or summer's noon
Sinks on the soul, like balm

On a parched wound.   And as the glow
Of sunlight's pride must perish ere
The stars can tremble, even so
Is many a modest beauty bid
To grace the staid night-season of the year,
Whom his bright day had hid ;

No longer overgrown with green,
But gemmed with rain and berry-crowned,
From each bare hedge the eye may glean
Soul-sustenance ;—enough to trace
One spray of white-veined ivy clinging round
An oak-tree's lichened base ;

Or roaming the chill fields among,
Where heavily the plough-team moves,
To hear the robin's slender song,
When fuller throats have ceased to strain,
Repeat to flowerless glades and mournful groves
Its simple sweet refrain ;

And nearing home, through leafless trees
To see the thin blue smoke ascend,
Where amid vine-clad cottages
Life slowly smoulders to its rest,
Each kindly-hearted swain a natural friend,
Each roof a human nest.

So would I praise the bounteous year,
And quickened by earth's close caress,
Would hold the lowliest weed more dear
Than all the laboured pomp of art ;
Eased of the city's crowded loneliness
Which chokes, yet starves, the heart ;

But strengthened from the living wells,
And nurtured on the wholesome fare
Of country sights and sounds and smells,
Would find beneath the greenwood bough
All that I loved in childhood unaware,
And love with worship now.

And let me at the last repose
Not where along unlovely ways
The roaring tide of trouble flows,
But where is heard the bleat of sheep,
And homely elms, that breathe of by-gone days,
Watch o'er the churchyard's sleep;

There by the sweet birds shall be said
My requiem, and death's garden wear
A look so kind, that unafraid
Children shall come to weave a wreath
Of daisies gathered from my grave, nor care
Who lieth underneath.

NOVEMBER

Mourner, who wanderest gray and mute
O'er mouldering leaves and fallen fruit,
Weep, unreproved !
Thou art not for thy sombre suit
The less beloved.

Welcome as April's bridal tears,
Or the ripe smile September wears,
Are thy grave eyes,
Made wistful with the agéd year's
Dim memories.

Thine are the dawns of solemn sheen,
Through interwoven branches seen,
         As when doth smite
Through some cathedral's carven screen
         The altar's light.

Thou lendest darkness to the yew,
To distant hills a deeper blue ;
         Thy footsteps wake
Mosses to flower, when flowers are few
         In leafless brake.

Fair as her liveliest summer dress
The beech's silver nakedness,
         When red and gold,
That robed her for the storm's caress,
         Her feet enfold.

Through steel-blue clouds a gleaming wedge
Strikes on the berry-jewelled hedge
         And dusky wood,
On osiers smooth and tawny sedge
         And streams in flood.

And as a child's light laugh beguiles
Sorrow to lose herself in smiles,
    The redbreast's lay
Maketh the woodland's silent aisles
    Seem almost gay.

'Tis good to watch the loose clouds driven,
When the broad south their web hath riven,
    Or pace again
Beneath a calm snow-burdened heaven
    The darkening lane,

Strewn with the maple's moth-like seeds,
And catch the scent of smouldering weeds
    O'er brown waves borne
Of fresh-ploughed loam and silent meads
    And cornfields shorn ;

'Tis good to feel thy teardrops fall
Upon the dead fern's quiet pall
    Of purple mist,
When frost for their snow-burial
    The wolds hath kissed ;

But best to watch—when death-like eve
The pensive landscape doth bereave
    Of short-lived day—
Thy great pathetic sunsets grieve
    Their hearts away.

CONSERVATION

Thou, who from many a spray forlorn
Its ruddy jewellery hast torn,
  Belovéd thrush !
From mountain-ash no need to fly,
At sight of me, to sanctuary
  Of laurel-bush.

Plunder thy fill !—my garden yet
Is sweet with stock and mignonette,
  With asters gay,
And of its plenty well can spare,
O prince of song, the frugal fare
  It doth purvey.

c

Soon will the dahlia's pride lie dead,
The sunflower droop his kingly head,
      And pinched with cold
The lordly hollyhock repine
For still September's mild sunshine
      And moon of gold.

Then winter with her wailful rains
Will weep o'er autumn's gaunt remains,
      Or watch them lie
Stark in the snow's sepulchral dress,
Entombed within a featureless
      Gray vault of sky.

But when I sigh, dear mottled thief,
For crocus-flower and lilac-leaf
      Delaying long,
The vanished splendour of the tree
Will glow again, conserved by thee,
      In glorious song.

ILLUSION

(Composed on observing that the rainbow, when steadily gazed at, disappears.)

WHEN in despite of care's dead weight,
And tarnished faith, and hope's decay,
A gladness stirs thee, delicate
As the first tremor of the spring
Or thrill of love's awakening,
Ask it not Whence—or it will shrink away.

So when the rainbow's transient smile
Cheereth heaven's gray and tearful face,
Look lightly on that tender wile ;
For if too hard, in joy's excess,
Thou gaze, the specious loveliness
Will fade as doth a dream, and leave no trace.

HAYESWATER

Enfolded in the mountain's naked arms,
  Where noonday wears a drearier look than night,
  And echo, like a shrinking anchorite,
  Wanders unseen, and shadowy strange alarms
Visit the soul ; there sunshine rarely warms
  The crags, but only random shafts of light
  Flit, while the black squalls shrilling from the
      height
  Shudder along the lake in scattering swarms.
Cradle of tempests, whence the whirlwind leaps
  To scourge the billows, till they writhe and rear
  Columns of hissing spray ; the wrinkled steeps
Scowl at the sullen moaning of the mere ;
  And luminous against the dale-side drear,
  Ghostlike, the rainstorm's scanty vesture sweeps.

HER FAITH

How quietly the cold hands keep,
Pressed to the gracious heart that loved their grace,
Poppies, unconscious of their resting-place,
    Emblems of dreamless sleep.

Around her the star-systems roll
Through wastes of silence.   Yet the enfolding Power,
That fashioned with such care a senseless flower,
    Will not forsake a soul.

LIGHT AND LOVE

Front not the sun ; or dazzled by his whiteness
Earth's face will seem expressionless and dim,
Features confused and beauty drowned in brightness ;
       But turn from him,
And thou wilt find familiar scenes and homely
Transfigured with a tender atmosphere ;
Scan not the source of all that makes earth comely ;
       Enough that light is here.

Question not love ; or pondering love's essence
The wonder of his glory will confound
Those fair effects that issue from his presence ;
       But look around,
And thou wilt find the narrowest prospect spacious,
And dark perplexities serenely clear ;
Scan not the source of all that makes life gracious ;
       Enough that love is here.

OUR SHAKESPEARE

To-night, where'er men boast thy native tongue,
    They crown thy brows anew with solemn bays,
    The cup in silence to thy memory raise,
    Imperial master of the feast of song—
In seemly silence—for what voice so strong,
    So sweet, as duly to declare thy praise?
    But we, who dwell where Arden yet arrays
    The oaks thou knew'st in green, where glides along
Gray Avon's peace, by many a gentle bend,
    Through homely pastures, and the bees still sip
    The flowers that heard thy footsteps—we may blend
Our homage with a sense of fellowship,
    May mark a kindlier smile illume thy lip,
    And feel thee less our sovereign than our friend.

PRO TEMPORE

Sɪᴄᴋ of the tumult, weary of the wail,
    That grateth where the city's breath is sour
    With greed's unclean disease, where children cower
    In noisome dens, and women gaunt and pale
Pollute their souls for bread, our hearts would fail
    But for the faith that in some wiser hour
    Men will possess in peace the world's rich bower ;
    Envy depart and righteousness prevail.
And yet, though other eyes than ours will see
    The far fulfilment of our larger hope,
    Justice ordains and pity pleads that we
Should cull one garland from the sunny slope
    Where ease reclines, to gladden those who grope
    In shades of want and sloughs of misery.

THE SILENT HARP

Poor harp, how desolate!—The loving hand,
  That wind-like wandered o'er thy tremulous strings,
  Culling sweet sheaves of sound or whisperings
  Æolian, at the Master's mute command
Drops lifeless. In that unresponsive land
  What music He from earthly sufferings
  Evoketh and the stress of mortal things,
  Wistful we seek but may not understand.
Yonder may dwell continual peace, but here
  All peace begetteth and is born of strife,
  And every smile is sister to a tear ;
Death only can the missing note supply
  That shall resolve the discord of this life ;
  Silence alone is perfect harmony.

THE IDEAL

Sorrow for him who evermore hath striven
To shape the perfect vision of his soul;
For gazing up into the face of heaven
    The falling snow seems foul.

MERRY AUTUMN

GOLDEN woodland, sea-blue sky,
Crests of cloud-waves tossed on high ;

Bouncing breezes, lustrous showers,
Leaves and berries gay as flowers ;

Purple storms in rainbow belt,
Morning frosts that flash and melt ;

Dawns arrayed in gorgeous light,
Dazzled earth in motley dight.

Robins flute a cheerful tune,
Orchards glow with apples strewn ;

Sunbeams bless the gathered sheaves,
Children chase the skipping leaves;

Buds grow plump in glossy sheath;—
Who dare call this rapture death?

Autumn's neither sick nor sad;
Spring's begotten; God is glad.

THE SEA

ELDEST of singers, never-silent sea,
    Whether in robe of gray or changeful green
    Thou chantest, or in mail of moonlight sheen,
    No ear hath learnt thine open mystery.
Companion of the world's wide grief, by thee
    We enter—gazing on thy tranquil mien,
    Or hearkening to the tempest's hollow threne—
    The echoing portals of eternity.
Whether on solemn shores advancing quires
    Of surpliced waves raise the resounding psalm,
    Or prostrate murmur prayer, thy voice avails
The pulse of man's disquietude to calm ;
    Mourner, whose long complaining never tires,
    Soother, whose consolation never fails.

IN THE HOUSE OF DEATH

I.

WITH tears they bring her babe to smile
  The last farewell; by childhood's grace,
In death's dark presence-hall awhile
      There shines a cloudless face.

Too young to know the awful bar
  That keeps him from those lips so white,
He wafts a baby kiss—sweet star
      Unconscious of the night—

And stretches dimpled hands to grasp
  The lilies on her breast, nor knows
How cold the hands their stems that clasp,
      How deep the breast's repose.

Poor helpless author of our dole,
　　Who ne'er shall lisp a mother's name,
God keep him, till he meet her soul
　　　　From whom he dearly came.

II.

Beside her fretful infant's cot
　　The father bows his stricken head ;
One lieth near, whose sleep will not
　　　　Be more disquieted.

The daylight faileth ; colourless
　　Are all things in the darkening room ;
Such nightfall doth his soul possess,
　　　　　Such dumb and hueless gloom.

With trembling hands the child he takes ;
　　He moans a verse the happy wife
Would croon ; then heaves a sob that shakes
　　　　The very roots of life.

O little arms around him curled,
    Cling closer to what love is left ;
Thou dost not know of what a world
    Of love thou art bereft.

THE DAWN OF SPRING

In the dead of winter's gloom,
When Earth in her shroud lay stark,
She dreamt that one day the lark
Would pierce with his sunny song
    Her snow-built tomb,
    And wake into bloom
The blossom that slept too long.

He is up!—and heaven's deep blue
Grew deeper for that last strain
Ere he dived to the warm-bosomed plain ;
And with what glad bound his voice
    Pealed forth anew,
    When again he flew
To the realms where the clouds rejoice !

D

He sang, as he stooped to his mate,
Of the glory of sun and sky;
But now the wild poesy,
That welcomes the first rainbow
　　And storms heaven's gate,
　　Is of joys that wait
On the breathing earth below.

The passionate hopes that swell
The great soul in his little breast
Not even his song hath expressed;
Nor the Muse, who has dipped a wing
　　In the living well
　　Of truth, can tell
The rapture of the spring;

It leaps in the gladsome air,
Like wine that hath long lain still
In the womb of earth, until

At a sunbeam's kiss it breaks
  Into frolic fair,
  And fragrance rare
From its dancing heart awakes ;

For April hath moved grim March
To smiles, and to tears the snow
That lurked by the black hedgerow ;
The brooks prattle loud of the showers ;
  And to breezes, that parch
  No more, the larch
Hath opened her crimson flowers.

Through the wayside herbage sere
A new-born green upheaves ;
The hornbeam's shrivelled leaves
Shudder for shame of their age ;
  For spring wastes no tear
  On the buried year,
But enjoyeth his heritage.

The coltsfoot, that never cringed
To the tyrannous east, doth make
Gay mock of his flight ; the brake
With the haze from its young buds shed
    Is dimly tinged,
    And the alder hath fringed
Its branches with tassels red.

Now gleam in the sun and dance
The gnats, frail brood of the calm ;
The bee, on the bee-like palm,
With his sultry summer sound
    And slow dalliance
    Doth disentrance
The butterfly underground.

The shining team doth crawl
Over the upland bare ;
Billows of loam, as the share

Upturneth the good brown land,
 Glistening fall,
 To be crumbled small
For the seed by the wind's broad hand.

The south her white-winged fleet
To the dappled hills hath driven;
The great warm heart of heaven,
Where love doth dwell, once more
 Is seen to beat,
 And its genial heat
Hath opened earth's every pore.

In the depths of the budding grove
Sweet fountains of feeling start;
They well in the old man's heart
As he lifteth his cottage latch,
 Where the courtly dove
 Makes murmuring love
To his lady on lichened thatch.

The rush of life, which thrills
The trees into tender sheen,
The sallow grass into green,
Is welcome as when the breath
    Of daffodils
    Fresh hope instils
In one who is watched by death.

O bliss! once more to feel
The native smell of earth,
Where the wheat has lowly birth
Or the violet's lip is curled,
    Through the sick soul steal,
    With power to heal
Like the hope of a better world;

To feel the soft caress
Of a breeze, foretelling May,
O'er the burdened bosom play

And fondle the troubled brow,
>
> While the sun doth dress
>
> In new loveliness
>
Each smooth sap-swollen bough !

His first hot kiss doth inspire
Earth's breast with a passion of joy ;
No more is she hard or coy ;
Her blood, benumbed so long,
>
> Is all afire
>
> With spring's desire,
>
And flames into flower and song.

Rejoice !—for care away
With the black east-wind has flown ;
Young mirth has mounted his throne ;
And love, no more heartsick
>
> At spring's delay,
>
> Resumes her sway ;
>
And the dead has become the quick.

ON THE MOUNTAIN

I SCALE the fortress where the winds keep ward
   . O'er health's unrifled hoard ;
Each footstep is an ecstasy ; my blood
   Leaps with the sparkling flood
Of sunshine from God's crystal chalice poured.
   Ascending I behold
   Earth's ancient scroll unfold ;
The mountain's naked shoulder screens from view
The valley of last night's expectant rest,
Whose hamlet, as the prospect grew,
   Shrank to a wood-wren's nest.
Panting with joyful toil at last I stand
   Where taintless breezes range,
An infant holding Nature by the hand,
A new-born creature, to myself most strange ;

Exalted to this sovereign height
I taste awhile an eagle's lone delight;
Then, as I scan
The Maker's outspread plan,
My humbled spirit kneels ·
And uncomplaining feels
The insignificance of man.
Around me slumber giant limbs ; below
The vapours crawl that curtain me from care ;
A stream unseen is heard to flow ;
The breast of peace lies bare ;
Reposing there,
I gaze along the avenues of air
To that which seems a sea beyond the sea,
The dim horizon of eternity.

FELLOW-CAPTIVES

How blest on earth's green lap to lie,
Escaped from town's captivity,
But that its smoke on evening gale
Far borne—this Eden's serpent-trail—
    Sullies the placid sky ;

Which else were stainless as the hue
Of those moss-cradled eggs, whose view
In quaint-cut hedge of town parterre
Drove me to seek the taintless air
    And unpolluted blue.

Not here, alas !—Full three leagues fled
From yon grim city, overhead
Hangs gloom, and silence doth appal
As in some stricken house where all
    The little ones lie dead.

What evil spell has power to hush
The rapture of the impassioned thrush?
What keeps his sable-suited peer
Dumb, and each dainty sonneteer
　　Of copse and lisping rush,

That follows summer o'er the foam?
Or why is heaven's eternal dome
Vacant of its high chorister?—
Nature, her music reft from her,
　　Is drearier than the home

Whose sadness slowly I regain
Through ever-deepening shades of pain,
As ever more the air grows sick
Where the dull miles of dismal brick
　　Spread like a loathsome blain;

My prison, and—God help you!—yours,
Poor little poets.　Man endures
The woe his own unwisdom yields,
Who lost the freedom of the fields,
　　Misled by his own lures;

But you, whose ditty's simple meed
Was still to pluck the thistle seed,
You, bolder finch of sanguine breast,
And you, small sir, with rosy crest—
    Cursed be the ruffian's greed

That mocked thy love-call, limed the spray
Where thou didst light to pipe thy lay,
Tore thee from all thou heldest dear,
To join thy captive song-mates here—
    A pitiful array

Of joy's own angels doomed to dwell
Pent in the city's weary hell;
For whisperings of the wind-swept wheat,
The clangour of the jostling street;
    For clover-breath, the smell

Of factory-fumes; for heaven's great ring,
Scarce space to prune an aching wing!
No more, ensconced in hawthorn flower,
To weave the wonder of their bower,
    Or feel the fluttering

Of those faint pulses soon to burst
Each fragile casket !—but accurst
With man's regard, exiled from nest,
Woodland and sky and all God's best,
To languish mid man's worst.

Is't not enough that lean and pale
His children pine, but he must hale
The happiest of created things,
Made free by God's great gift of wings,
To share his crowded jail ?

A STORM SONG

CHASTEN the land, O wind ;
   Hurl autumn from his throne ;
Be pitiless, be blind,
   And let the forest groan ;
The forest's quickened life
   Will bless thee yet ; for thou
Art God's keen pruning-knife
   That lops each withered bough.

Chasten the land, O war ;
   Consume the false and frail
With fire of thy red star,
   And let the nation wail ;
Redeemed by sore distress
   From rottenness of soul,
'Twill live some day to bless
   The storm that made it whole.

THE TRYST

THE stars are faint and few,
The zenith yet is blue;

By daylight still is seen
The orchard's tender green,

Whose snowy bloom doth rest
As clouds on heaven's breast;

But clear and full and high
The moon enchants the sky.

When day and moonlight meet
My heart doth strangely beat;

For when their lips have kissed,
I keep my silent tryst

With One, to whom alone
My inmost heart is known.

Her footsteps then are heard
When sleeping leaves are stirred ;

Her eyes more tender are
Than twilight's only star ;

She breathes as when the plane
Is fragrant after rain ;

Her voice is that deep speech
Which music yearns to reach.

To her pure lips I clung
When boyhood's leaf was young ;

Her soul possessed the maid
When love was first afraid ;

But now that love is bold,
The gray consumes the gold.

Sweet is the sultry noon
Of lusty full-blown June,

And sweet the golden fruit
Of love's accomplished suit ;

But sweeter twilight's hour
And love's unfolding flower.

TO THE COWSLIP

OF all spring joys, the dearest is
To drink thy breath again,
Freshest of flowers ;
The bluebell lights the copse,
The primrose paves the glen,
But thy frank beauty overtops
In open fields
The new-born grass, to meet the kiss
Of sun and wind and showers,
And yields
Spring's essence from those five red drops
That dyed the breast of Imogen.

Sun-freckled art thou, as the child
    Who kneeleth down to snap
      Thy sturdy stem,
  And fill with thy pure gold
    Her snowy-aproned lap,
White treasury of wealth untold ;
    Deftly she makes,
In bountiful profusion piled,
    A regal ball of them,
      And takes
For sceptre one that high doth hold
His head in pride of April sap.

My earliest love of flowers, how good
    To lay my sunburnt face
      In grass so lush
  It shames the name of green,
  And fold in one embrace
The clustered heads of all I glean,

And kiss the pure
Warm lips of that fair sisterhood,
Or 'mid their golden flush
Immure
The splendour of some cowslip queen
Who reigned apart in loftier grace.

Then home to sleep by Avon stream,
Cheered by the honest wine
Of cowslip flowers ;
So pure a draught alone
Gives slumber so divine ;
All night I breathe the sweet air blown
O'er fields thick starred
With cowslip constellations, dream
Of gold-embrasured towers
That guard
Some fay for whom the bees make moan,
While cowslips by my cheek recline.

A NOVEMBER PARABLE

AH! piteous sight!
While yet the weird moonlight
Wove o'er the land her numbing spell,
Not a leaf fell
To break the crystal silence of the night.

But since the frost-subduing sun
His azure seigniory
From the horizon-mist hath won,
Whence his white troops in massive splendour loom,
The stricken leaves unceasingly
Down flutter to their tomb.

So one who long hath borne
Grief's bitter cold,
Till faith has failed and hope herself grown old,
Endureth till the last chill hour is fled,
But at the flash of joy's forgotten morn
Drops dead.

RUSSIA

(December, 1891)

As one, who finds the foe he sought to slay
   Prostrate within the shadow of the tomb,
   Forgets his wrath, so, grieving for thy doom,
   Huge wrestler with starvation, we would lay
Our ancient grudge aside. The heavens are gray
   With pitiless calm, and walls of winter loom
   Around thy blighted plains; while he, to whom
   Thou liftest ignorant hands, sits far away,
Unenvied prisoner to a fatal throne,
   Spellbound, with nerveless arm and eye askance.
   So vast thy misery, one hope alone
Rests—that, all else too weak, it may betide
   Hunger's grim hand by dreadful paths will guide
   Thy laggard feet to thy deliverance.

REQUIESCAT

(October 6th, 1892)

PEACE !—for no feebler voice avails to sing
The loss of him who best hath sung of loss.
    Nature herself with folded wing
    Stood mute ; the great night held its breath ;
    Solemn the moonlight watched across
    The mournful calm of summer's grave,
    When reverently the hand of death
Earth's transitory chaplet took, and gave
       An everlasting wreath.

    Peace !—let no sacrilegious strain
       Discordantly profane

The sanctuary of silence where he lies,
Heedless of human worship, with the glow
Of God's white lamp upon the closéd eyes
   And cold imperial brow.
  Nor let a hasty hand presume
To lift the hallowed laurel from his tomb.

∴

POESY

He hears the music of his heart,
　　But knows not whence the breath is blown ;
It comes from regions far apart,
　　With power beyond his own.

A presence at his side alights,
　　A whisper at his ear is heard ;
Amazed he takes the pen, and writes
　　The inevitable word.

TO THE REDBREAST

SWEET minstrel of the homes of men,
Waylayer of my early walk,
  Stay till this dahlia stalk
    Is tied, and then
      We'll talk.

There, pretty gossip!—now, come near,
With jaunty tail, and head awry ;
  Thou least, of things that fly,
    Hast need to fear
      Man's eye.

A gracious legend guardeth thee,
My robin, with a hallowed name ;
  And trustfulness so tame
    Puts cruelty
      To shame.

No prison waits for thee, dear ; who,
Of all the joy-deserted throng
  Who buy a captive song,
    Would dare to do
      Thee wrong ?

Yes, I remember well the nest,
Six little bosoms brown-bespecked—
  O tender architect—
    And then each breast
      Fire-flecked.

Yes ; summer's gone ; but what of that ?
Now that her timid devotees
  Are fled across the seas,
    We two can chat
      At ease.

We love to hear the bold wind blow,
To see his random might deflower
  The rocking elms, that shower
    Their golden snow
      Where cower

The sheep behind a shivering hedge ;
We love the huddling clouds that rove
　　O'er the blue plain above
　　　The horizon's edge ;
　　　　We love

The tones, by moisture richly dyed,
Of winter's warm-hued nakedness,
　　When south winds blow, not less
　　　Than autumn's pride
　　　　Of dress.

Then every voice but thine doth cease,
While He, Who teacheth all to sing,
　　Is darkly pondering
　　　His masterpiece,
　　　　The spring.

As faintly through the gloom and damp
That fills some melancholy shrine,
　　When evening's brows decline,
　　　A single lamp
　　　　Doth shine ;

So, when the mournful sunbeams slant
Where summer lieth sepulchred,
A throb of hope, bright bird,
In thy spare chant
Is heard.

ESTRANGEMENT

No comfort in the world remains
    When love is fled;
'Tis but a coffin that contains
    The dead, the dead.

The unregarding wind sweeps by,
    Blank stares the heaven;
Indifferent along the sky
    The mist is driven.

Nursing their sorrow to and fro
    The sad boughs toss;
Winter bewaileth her own woe,
    And not our loss.

O Nature, who dost give relief
  To joy's full heart,
Thou, when the soul is spent with grief,
  An alien art.

.

THE LARK IN AUTUMN

THE day's long splendour dies
   A lingering death.—How still
The sea of country lies
   Around this island hill.

The nestling sunbeams creep
   Beneath the boughs ; the gold
Fades into gray, and sleep
   Descends on vale and wold.

God gave His wine all day,
   Eve brings His healing balm ;
Care perished far away
   In yonder purple calm.

F

Joy's river, that hath run
   So swiftly, now doth flow
Toward the setting sun
   With gathered fulness slow.—

But what bright spirit there
   Leaps into music?—Hark!
The poet of the air,
   The sky's own soul,—the lark!

His song the dayspring seems,
   His pinions, as they soar,
Are lustrous with the beams
   That light the land no more.

So often, at life's close,
   A thrill of youth's delight
Invades its gray repose,
   And greets the dawn of night.

MY STUDY

LET others strive for wealth or praise
        Who care to win ;
I count myself full blest, if He,
Who made my study fair to see,
Grant me but length of quiet days
        To muse therein.

Its walls, with peach and cherry clad,
        From yonder wold
Unbosomed, seem as if thereon
September sunbeams ever shone ;
They make the air look warm and glad
        When winds are cold.

Around its door a clematis
         Her arms doth tie ;
Through leafy lattices I view
Its endless corridors of blue
Curtained with clouds ; its ceiling is
         The marbled sky.

A verdant carpet smoothly laid
         Doth oft invite
My silent steps ; thereon the sun
With silver thread of dew hath spun
Devices rare—the warp of shade,
         The weft of light.

Here dwell my chosen books, whose leaves
         With healing breath
The ache of discontent assuage,
And speak from each illumined page
The patience that my soul reprieves
         From inward death ;

Some perish with a season's wind,
      And some endure ;
One robes itself in snow, and one
In raiment of the rising sun
Bordered with gold ;—in all I find
      God's signature.

As on my grassy couch I lie,
      From hedge and tree
Musicians pipe ; or if the heat
Subdue the birds, one crooneth sweet
Whose labour is a lullaby,—
      The slumbrous bee.

The sun my work doth overlook
      With searching light ;
The serious moon, the flickering star,
My midnight lamp and candle are ;
A soul unhardened is the book
      Wherein I write.

There labouring, my heart is eased
    Of every care ;
Yet often wonderstruck I stand,
With earnest gaze but idle hand,
Abashed—for God Himself is pleased
    To labour there.

Ashamed my faultful task to spell,
    I watch how grows
The Master's perfect colour-scheme
Of sunset, or His simpler dream
Of moonlight, or that miracle
    We name a rose.

There, in the lap of pure content,
    I still would keep
The sabbath of a soul at rest ;
Nor could I wish a close more blest
Than there, when life's bright day is spent,
    To fall asleep.

TO THE NEGLECTED MUSE

HIGH priestess of the temple where my soul
　　Would daily kneel!
　When happier singers make appeal
　　For grace, and I
Neglect thy service, chide not, but condole
　　With thy poor votary.

Forget thee?—ah! this morning, when soft flights
　　　Of sea-born cloud
　Sailed o'er the unregarding crowd
　　In that dense mart
Where I am bound, remembrance of thy rites
　　Was torment to my heart;

And now returning through the city's roar,
With toil opprest,
And marking how the liquid west
From cloud is free,
Save one smooth bank that seems the printless shore
Of some untraversed sea,

I groan to think how twilight slowly fills
The spacious vale
Where I would watch with thee, how pale
Thy star-lamp shines,
While sunset dies beyond the solemn hills
And nightfall stirs the pines.

Still would I seek thee by the stream which flows
Through that sweet shire,
Where he who lightliest touched the lyre
Is laid asleep,
Till with its sister flood it found repose
In slumber of the deep.

There would I follow thee, would shut my ears
To pleasure's call ;
But duty holdeth me in thrall,
My days rush by,
And rarely through the driving rack appears
A space of quiet sky.

How should I sing when all my heart is kept
In bondage, vexed
With strife, and all my brain perplexed
With many a thread
Of tangled thought ; I have no song ; accept,
O Muse, my sighs instead.

Forget thee ?—if my fingers could unclasp
The lyre, and seize
Life's cup, and drain it to the lees,
Then might I set
My heart no more on joy beyond my grasp,
Ah ! then I might forget.

G

Once I had thought in that fair company
To find a place,
Who daily tend before thy face
The sacred fire ;
But love and care with one another vie
To thrust me from the quire.

Yet sometimes 'mid the city's glare and grime,
Far from thy sight,
I stand thy silent acolyte ;
Enough for me ;
I ask not thy regard, but only time,
Dear saint, to worship thee.

OTHER BOOKS BY ALFRED HAYES

THE DEATH OF SAINT LOUIS
>   PRIVATELY PRINTED, 1886   [*Out of print*

THE LAST CRUSADE AND OTHER POEMS
>   FIRST EDITION, 1887
>   SECOND EDITION, 1887
>
>   Birmingham, CORNISH BROS.

DAVID WESTREN
>   FIRST EDITION, 1888
>   SECOND EDITION, 1888
>
>   Birmingham, CORNISH BROS.

THE MARCH OF MAN AND OTHER POEMS
>   FIRST EDITION, 1891
>   SECOND EDITION, 1892
>
>   London, MACMILLAN & Co.

FROM MIDLAND MEADOWS
>   (Included in " A Fellowship in Song "), 1893
>
>   Rugby, GEORGE E. OVER
>   London, ELKIN MATHEWS & JOHN LANE
>   [*Out of print*

*Turnbull & Spears, Printers,
Edinburgh.*

List of Books

IN

Belles Lettres

JOHN LANE PUB
LISHER of BELLES
LETTRES. 🐦 🐦 🐦
The BODLEY HEAD
VIGO St LONDON

All the Books in this Catalogue
are Published at Net Prices

1894

Telegraphic Address
Bodleian, London

List of Books

IN

BELLES LETTRES

(Including some Transfers)

Published by John Lane

𝔗𝔥𝔢 𝔅𝔬𝔡𝔩𝔢𝔶 𝔥𝔢𝔞𝔡

Vigo Street, London, W.

N.B.—The Authors and Publisher reserve the right of reprinting any book in this list if a new edition is called for, except in cases where a stipulation has been made to the contrary, and of printing a separate edition of any of the books for America irrespective of the numbers to which the English editions are limited. The numbers mentioned do not include copies sent to the public libraries, nor those sent for review.

Most of the books are published simultaneously in England and America, and in many instances the names of the American publishers are appended.

ADAMS (FRANCIS).
  ESSAYS IN MODERNITY. Cr. 8vo. 5s. *net.*   [*Shortly.*
  Chicago: Stone & Kimball.

ADAMS (FRANCIS).
  A CHILD OF THE AGE. Cr. 8vo. 3s. 6d. *net.*
   (*See* KEYNOTES SERIES.)   [*Immediately.*
  Boston: Roberts Bros.

ALLEN (GRANT).
THE LOWER SLOPES : A Volume of Verse. With title-page
and cover design by J. ILLINGWORTH KAY. 600 copies.
Cr. 8vo.   5s.   net.
Chicago : Stone & Kimball.

ALLEN (GRANT).
THE WOMAN WHO DID.   Cr. 8vo.   3s. 6d. net.
(*See* KEYNOTES SERIES.)   [*In rapid preparation.*
Boston : Roberts Bros.

BEARDSLEY (AUBREY).
THE STORY OF VENUS AND TANNHÄUSER, in which is
set forth an exact account of the Manner of State held
by Madam Venus, Goddess and Meretrix, under the
famous Hörselberg, and containing the adventures of
Tannhäuser in that place, his repentance, his journeying
to Rome, and return to the loving Mountain. By
AUBREY BEARDSLEY. With 20 full-page illustrations,
numerous ornaments, and a cover from the same hand.
Sq. 16mo.   10s. 6d. net.   [*In preparation.*

BEECHING (Rev. H. C.).
IN A GARDEN : Poems.   With a specially-designed title-
page.   Cr. 8vo.   5s. net.   [*In preparation.*

BENSON (ARTHUR CHRISTOPHER).
LYRICS.   Fcap. 8vo.   5s. net.   [*In rapid preparation.*

BROTHERTON (MARY).
ROSEMARY FOR REMEMBRANCE. With title-page designed
by WALTER WEST.   Fcap. 8vo.   5s. net.
                                    [*In rapid preparation.*

DALMON (C. W.).
SONG FAVOURS.   With a specially-designed title-page.
Sq. 16mo.   4s. 6d. net.   [*In preparation.*

D'ARCY (ELLA).
A VOLUME OF STORIES.   Cr. 8vo.   3s. 6d. net.
                                    [*In preparation.*
(*See* KEYNOTES SERIES.)
Boston : Roberts Bros.

DAVIDSON (JOHN).
> PLAYS: An Unhistorical Pastoral; A Romantic Farce
> Bruce, a Chronicle Play; Smith, a Tragic Farce;
> Scaramouch in Naxos, a Pantomime. With a frontis·
> piece and cover design by AUBREY BEARDSLEY.
> Printed at the Ballantyne Press. 500 copies. Sm. 4to.
> 7s. 6d. net.
> *Chicago: Stone & Kimball.*

DAVIDSON (JOHN).
> FLEET ST. ECLOGUES. 2nd edition. Fcap. 8vo., buckram.
> 5s. net.

DAVIDSON (JOHN).
> A RANDOM ITINERARY AND A BALLAD. With a frontis-
> piece and title-page by LAURENCE HOUSMAN. 600
> copies. Fcap. 8vo., Irish linen. 5s. net.
> *Boston: Copeland & Day.*

DAVIDSON (JOHN).
> THE NORTH WALL. Fcap. 8vo. 2s. 6d. net.

> *The few remaining copies transferred by the Author to the
> present Publisher.*

DAVIDSON (JOHN).
> BALLADS AND SONGS. With title-page designed by WALTER
> WEST. Fcap. 8vo., buckram. 5s. net.
> *Boston: Copeland & Day.*

DE TABLEY (LORD).
> POEMS, DRAMATIC AND LYRICAL. By JOHN LEICESTER
> WARREN (Lord De Tabley). Illustrations and cover
> design by C. S. RICKETTS. 2nd edition. Cr. 8vo.
> 7s. 6d. net.

DE TABLEY (LORD).
> NEW POEMS. Cr. 8vo. 5s. net.　　　　　*[In preparation.*

EGERTON (GEORGE).
> KEYNOTES. 6th edition. Cr. 8vo. 3s. 6d. net.
> (*See* KEYNOTES SERIES.)
> *Boston: Roberts Bros.*

EGERTON (GEORGE).
  DISCORDS. Cr. 8vo. 3s. 6d. net.
    (*See* KEYNOTES SERIES.)   [*In rapid preparation.*
  Boston: Roberts Bros.

EGERTON (GEORGE).
  YOUNG OFEG'S DITTIES. A translation from the Swedish
    of OLA HANSSON. Cr. 8vo. 3s. 6d. net.
                                        [*In preparation.*
FARR (FLORENCE).
  THE DANCING FAUN. Cr. 8vo. 3s. 6d. net.
    (*See* KEYNOTES SERIES.)
  Boston: Roberts Bros.

FLETCHER (J. S.).
  THE WONDERFUL WAPENTAKE. By "A SON OF THE
    SOIL." With 18 full-page illustrations on Japanese
    vellum, by J. A. SYMINGTON. Cr. 8vo. 5s. 6d. net.
                                        [*In rapid preparation.*
GALE (NORMAN).
  ORCHARD SONGS, with title-page and cover design by
    J. ILLINGWORTH KAY. Fcap. 8vo., Irish linen.
    5s. net.
  Also a special edition, limited in number, on hand-made
    paper, bound in English vellum. £1. 1s. net.
  New York: G. P. Putnam's Sons.

GARNETT (RICHARD).
  POEMS. With title-page by J. ILLINGWORTH KAY. 350
    copies. Cr. 8vo. 5s. net.
  Boston: Copeland & Day.

GOSSE (EDMUND).
  THE LETTERS OF THOMAS LOVELL BEDDOES. Now
    first edited. Pott 8vo. 5s. net.
  New York: Macmillan & Co.

GRAHAME (KENNETH).
  PAGAN PAPERS: A VOLUME OF ESSAYS. With title-page
    by AUBREY BEARDSLEY. Fcap. 8vo. 5s. net.
  Chicago: Stone & Kimball.

GREENE (G. A.).
ITALIAN LYRISTS OF TO-DAY. Translations in the original metres from about 35 living Italian poets ; with bibliographical and biographical notes. Cr. 8vo. 5s. *net.*
New York: Macmillan & Co.

GREENWOOD (FREDERICK).
IMAGINATION IN DREAMS. Cr. 8vo. 5s. *net.*
[*In rapid preparation.*

HAKE (T. GORDON).
A SELECTION FROM HIS POEMS. Edited by Mrs. MEYNELL, with a portrait after D. G. ROSSETTI, and a cover design by GLEESON WHITE. Cr. 8vo. 5s. *net.*
Chicago: Stone & Kimball.

HARLAND (HENRY).
THE BOHEMIAN GIRL, AND OTHER STORIES. Cr. 8vo. 3s. 6d. *net.* (*See* KEYNOTES SERIES). [*In preparation.*
Boston: Roberts Bros.

HAYES (ALFRED).
THE VALE OF ARDEN, AND OTHER POEMS. With a title-page designed by E. H. NEW. Fcap. 8vo. 3s. 6d. *net.* [*In preparation.*

HEINEMANN (WILLIAM).
THE FIRST STEP : A Dramatic Moment. Sm. 4to. 3s. 6d. *net.* [*Immediately.*

HOPPER (NORA).
BALLADS IN PROSE. With a title-page and cover by WALTER WEST. Sq. 16mo. 5s. *net.*
Boston: Roberts Bros.

IRVING (LAURENCE).
GODEFROI AND YOLANDE : A Play. With 3 illustrations by AUBREY BEARDSLEY. Sm. 4to. 5s. *net.*
[*In preparation.*

JAMES (W. P.).
ROMANTIC PROFESSIONS : A volume of Essays. With title-page designed by J. ILLINGWORTH KAY. Cr. 8vo. 5s. *net.*
New York: Macmillan & Co.

JOHNSON (LIONEL).
THE ART OF THOMAS HARDY.   Six Essays, with etched
   portrait by WM. STRANG, and Bibliography by JOHN
   LANE.   Cr. 8vo.   Buckram.   5*s. 6d. net.*
      Also 150 copies, large paper, with proofs of the
      portrait.   £1. 1*s. net.*   [*Just published.*
   New York: Dodd, Mead & Co
JOHNSON (PAULINE).
WHITE WAMPUM : Poems.   Cr. 8vo.   5*s. net.*
                                          [*In preparation.*
JOHNSTONE (C. E.).
BALLADS OF BOY AND BEAK.   Fcap. 8vo.   2*s. 6d. net.*
                                          [*In preparation.*
KEYNOTES SERIES.
Each volume with specially-designed title-page by AUBREY
   BEARDSLEY.   Cr. 8vo. cloth.   3*s. 6d. net.*
Vol.   I. KEYNOTES.   By GEORGE EGERTON.
                                  [*Sixth Edition now ready.*
Vol.   II. THE DANCING FAUN.   By FLORENCE FARR.
Vol.   III. POOR FOLK.   Translated from the Russian of
      F. DOSTOIEVSKY by LENA MILMAN, with a
      preface by GEORGE MOORE.
Vol.   IV. A CHILD OF THE AGE.   By FRANCIS ADAMS.
Vol.   V. THE GREAT GOD PAN AND THE INMOST
      LIGHT.   By ARTHUR MACHEN.
                                  [*About December 1st.*
Vol.   VI. DISCORDS.   By GEORGE EGERTON.
                                  [*About December 1st.*
   The following are in rapid preparation :—
Vol.   VII. PRINCE ZALESKI.   By M. P. SHIEL.
Vol. VIII. THE WOMAN WHO DID.   By GRANT ALLEN.
Vol.   IX. WOMEN'S TRAGEDIES.   By H. D. LOWRY.
Vol.   X. THE BOHEMIAN GIRL AND OTHER STORIES.
      By HENRY HARLAND.
Vol.   XI. A VOLUME OF STORIES.   By H. B. MARRIOTT
      WATSON.
Vol.   XII. A VOLUME OF STORIES.   By ELLA D'ARCY.
Boston : Roberts Bros.

LEATHER (R. K.).
VERSES. 250 copies, fcap. 8vo. 3s. *net.*
Transferred by the Author to the present Publisher.

LE GALLIENNE (RICHARD).
PROSE FANCIES, with a portrait of the Author, by WILSON
STEER. Third edition. Cr. 8vo., purple cloth, uniform
with "The Religion of a Literary Man." 5s. *net.*
Also a limited large paper edition. 12s. 6d. *net.*
New York: G. P. Putnam's Sons.

LE GALLIENNE (RICHARD).
THE BOOK BILLS OF NARCISSUS. An account rendered
by RICHARD LE GALLIENNE. Third edition, cr. 8vo.,
purple cloth, uniform with "The Religion of a Literary
Man." 3s. 6d. *net.*   [*In rapid preparation.*

LE GALLIENNE (RICHARD).
ENGLISH POEMS. Third edition, cr. 8vo. purple cloth,
uniform with "The Religion of a Literary Man."
5s *net.*
Boston : Copeland & Day.

LE GALLIENNE (RICHARD).
GEORGE MEREDITH : Some Characteristics ; with a Biblio-
graphy (much enlarged) by JOHN LANE, portrait, &c.
Fourth edition, cr. 8vo., purple cloth, uniform with
"The Religion of a Literary Man." 5s. 6d. *net.*

LE GALLIENNE (RICHARD).
THE RELIGION OF A LITERARY MAN. 5th thousand.
Cr. 8vo., purple cloth. 3s. 6d. *net.*
Also a special rubricated edition on hand-made paper.
8vo. 10s. 6d. *net.*
New York: G. P. Putnam's Sons.

LOWRY (H. D.).
WOMEN'S TRAGEDIES. Cr. 8vo. 3s. 6d. *net.*
(*See* KEYNOTES SERIES.)   [*In preparation.*
Boston : Roberts Bros.

LUCAS (WINIFRED).
A VOLUME OF POEMS. Fcap. 8vo. 4s. 6d. net.
[In preparation.

MACHEN (ARTHUR).
THE GREAT GOD PAN AND THE INMOST LIGHT. Cr. 8vo.
3s. 6d. net.
(See KEYNOTES SERIES.)   [In rapid preparation.
Boston : Roberts Bros.

MARZIALS (THEO.).
THE GALLERY OF PIGEONS, AND OTHER POEMS. Post 8vo.
4s. 6d. net.   [Very few remain.
Transferred by the Author to the present Publisher.

MEREDITH (GEORGE).
THE FIRST PUBLISHED PORTRAIT OF THIS AUTHOR,
engraved on the wood by W. BISCOMBE GARDNER,
after the painting by G. F. WATTS. Proof copies on
Japanese vellum, signed by painter and engraver.
£1. 1s. net.

MEYNELL (MRS.) (ALICE C. THOMPSON).
POEMS. 2nd edition. Fcap. 8vo. 3s. 6d. net. A few of
the 50 large paper copies (1st edition) remain. 12s. 6d.
net.

MEYNELL (MRS.).
THE RHYTHM OF LIFE, AND OTHER ESSAYS. 2nd edition.
Fcap. 8vo. 3s. 6d. net. A few of the 50 large paper
copies (1st edition) remain. 12s. 6d. net.

MILLER (JOAQUIN).
THE BUILDING OF THE CITY BEAUTIFUL. Fcap. 8vo.
With a decorated cover. 5s. net.   [Just published.
Chicago : Stone & Kimball.

MILMAN (LENA).
POOR FOLK. Translated from the Russian of F. DOS-
TOIEVSKY. (See KEYNOTES SERIES.) Cr. 8vo. 3s. 6d.
net.
Boston : Roberts Bros.

MONKHOUSE (ALLAN).
BOOKS AND PLAYS : A VOLUME OF ESSAYS ON MEREDITH, BORROW, IBSEN, AND OTHERS. 400 copies. Cr. 8vo. 5s. *net*.
Philadelphia : J. B. Lippincott Co. ▾

NESBIT (E.).
A VOLUME OF POEMS. Cr. 8vo. 5s. *net*.
[*In preparation.*

NETTLESHIP (J. T.).
ROBERT BROWNING. Essays and Thoughts. 3rd edition, with a portrait. Cr. 8vo. 5s. 6d. *net*.
[*In rapid preparation.*
New York : Chas. Scribner's Sons.

NOBLE (JAS. ASHCROFT).
THE SONNET IN ENGLAND, AND OTHER ESSAYS. Title-page and cover design by AUSTIN YOUNG. 600 copies. Cr. 8vo. 5s. *net*. Also 50 copies L.P. 12s. 6d. *net*.

O'SHAUGHNESSY (ARTHUR).
HIS LIFE AND HIS WORK. With selections from his Poems. By LOUISE CHANDLER MOULTON. Portrait and cover design. Fcap. 8vo. 5s. *net*.
[*Just published.*
Chicago : Stone & Kimball.

OXFORD CHARACTERS.
A series of lithographed Portraits by WILL ROTHENSTEIN, with text by F. YORK POWELL and others. To be issued monthly in term. Each number will contain two portraits. Parts I. to V. ready. 200 sets only, folio, wrapper, 5s. *net* per part ; 25 special large paper sets containing proof impressions of the portraits signed by the artist, 10s. 6d. *net* per part.

PETERS (WM. THEODORE).
POSIES OUT OF RINGS. Sq. 16mo. 3s. 6d. *net*.
[*In preparation.*

PLARR (*VICTOR*).
A VOLUME OF POEMS. Cr. 8vo. 5s. *net*.
[*In preparation*.

RICKETTS (*C. S.*) *AND C. H. SHANNON*.
HERO AND LEANDER. BY CHRISTOPHER MARLOWE and
GEORGE CHAPMAN. With borders, initials, and illus-
trations designed and engraved on the wood by C. S.
RICKETTS and C. H. SHANNON. Bound in English
vellum and gold. 200 copies only. 35s. *net*.
Boston: Copeland & Day.

RHYS (*ERNEST*).
A LONDON ROSE AND OTHER RHYMES. With title-page
designed by SELWYN IMAGE. 350 copies. Cr. 8vo.
5s. *net*.
New York: Dodd, Mead, & Co.

SHIEL (*M. P.*).
PRINCE ZALESKI. Cr 8vo. 3s. 6d. *net*.
(*See* KEYNOTES SERIES.)   [*In preparation*.
Boston: Roberts Bros.

STREET (*G. S*).
THE AUTOBIOGRAPHY OF A BOY. Passages selected by
his friend, G. S. S. With title-page designed by
C. W. FURSE. Fcap. 8vo. 3s. 6d. *net*.
[*Fourth Edition now ready*.
Philadelphia: J. B. Lippincott Co.

SYMONS (*ARTHUR*).
A NEW VOLUME OF POEMS. Cr. 8vo. 5s. *net*.
[*In preparation*.

THOMPSON (*FRANCIS*).
A VOLUME OF POEMS. With frontispiece, title-page, and
cover design by LAURENCE HOUSMAN. 4th edition.
Pott 4to. 5s. *net*.
Boston: Copeland & Day.

TREE (H. BEERBOHM).
THE IMAGINATIVE FACULTY: a Lecture delivered at the
Royal Institution. With portrait of Mr. TREE from
an unpublished drawing by the Marchioness of Granby.
Fcap. 8vo., boards. 2s. 6d net.

TYNAN HINKSON (KATHARINE).
CUCKOO SONGS. With title-page and cover design by
LAURENCE HOUSMAN. Fcap. 8vo. 5s. net.
Boston: Copeland & Day.

TYNAN HINKSON (KATHARINE).
MIRACLE PLAYS.   [In preparation.

WATSON (H. B. MARRIOTT).
A VOLUME OF STORIES. Cr. 8vo. 3s. 6d. net.
(See KEYNOTES SERIES.)   [In preparation.
Boston: Roberts Bros.

WATSON (WILLIAM).
ODES, AND OTHER POEMS. Fcap. 8vo. 4s. 6d. net.
                              [About December 1st.
New York: Macmillan & Co.

WATSON (WILLIAM).
THE ELOPING ANGELS: A CAPRICE. 2nd edition. Sq.
16mo, buckram. 3s. 6d. net.
New York: Macmillan & Co.

WATSON (WILLIAM).
EXCURSIONS IN CRITICISM : BEING SOME PROSE RECREA-
TIONS OF A RHYMER. 2nd edition, cr. 8vo. 5s. net.
New York: Macmillan & Co.

WATSON (WILLIAM).
THE PRINCE'S QUEST, AND OTHER POEMS. With a
bibliographical note added. 2nd edition, fcap. 8vo.
4s. 6d. net.

WATTS (THEODORE).
POEMS. Cr. 8vo. 5s. net.   [In preparation.
There will also be an Edition de Luxe of this volume printed
at the Kelmscott Press.

WHARTON (H. T.).

SAPPHO. Memoir, text, selected renderings, and a literal translation by HENRY THORNTON WHARTON. With three illustrations, fcap. 8vo.   7s. 6d. net.
[*In preparation.*

WILDE (OSCAR).

THE SPHINX. A Poem. Decorated throughout in line and colour and bound in a design by CHARLES RICKETTS. 250 copies, £2. 2s. net. 25 copies large paper, £5. 5s. net.
Boston : Copeland & Day.

WILDE (OSCAR).

The incomparable and ingenious history of Mr. W. H., being the true secret of Shakespear's sonnets, now for the first time here fully set forth. With initial letters and cover design by CHARLES RICKETTS. 500 copies, 10s. 6d. net. Also 50 copies large paper, 21s. net.
[*In preparation.*

WILDE (OSCAR).

DRAMATIC WORKS, now printed for the first time. With a specially-designed binding to each volume, by CHARLES SHANNON. 500 copies, sm. 4to., 7s. 6d. net per vol. Also 50 copies large paper, 15s. net per vol.

Vol. I. LADY WINDERMERE'S FAN. A comedy in four acts. [*Out of print.*

Vol. II. A WOMAN OF NO IMPORTANCE. A comedy in four acts. [*Just published.*

Vol. III. THE DUCHESS OF PADUA. A blank verse tragedy in five acts. [*Very shortly.*

Boston : Copeland & Day.

WILDE (OSCAR).

SALOME . A Tragedy in one act, done into English, with 10 illustrations, title-page, tail-piece, and cover design by AUBREY BEARDSLEY. 500 copies, sm. 4to. 15s. net. Also 100 copies large paper, 30s. net.
Boston : Copeland & Day.

The Yellow Book.

An Illustrated Quarterly.

VOL. I. Fourth Edition, pott 4to., 272 *pp.*, 15 *Illustrations, Decorative Cloth Cover, price* 5s. *net.*

The Letterpress by MAX BEERBOHM, A. C. BENSON, HUBERT CRACKANTHORPE, ELLA D'ARCY, JOHN DAVIDSON, GEORGE EGERTON, RICHARD GARNETT, EDMUND GOSSE, HENRY HARLAND, JOHN OLIVER HOBBES, HENRY JAMES, RICHARD LE GALLIENNE, GEORGE MOORE, GEORGE SAINTSBURY, FRED M. SIMPSON, ARTHUR SYMONS, WILLIAM WATSON, ARTHUR WAUGH.

The Illustrations by SIR FREDERIC LEIGHTON, P.R.A., AUBREY BEARDSLEY, R. ANNING BELL. CHARLES W. FURSE, LAURENCE HOUSMAN, J. T. NETTLESHIP, JOSEPH PENNELL, WILL ROTHENSTEIN, WALTER SICKERT.

VOL. II. Third Edition, pott 4to., 364 *pp.*, 23 *Illustrations, with a New Decorative Cloth Cover, price* 5s. *net.*

The Literary Contributions by FREDERICK GREENWOOD, ELLA D'ARCY, CHARLES WILLEBY, JOHN DAVIDSON, HENRY HARLAND, DOLLIE RADFORD, CHARLOTTE M. MEW, AUSTIN DOBSON, V., O., C. S., KATHARINE DE MATTOS. PHILIP GILBERT HAMERTON, RONALD CAMPBELL MACFIE, DAUPHIN MEUNIER, KENNETH GRAHAME, NORMAN GALE, NETTA SYRETT, HUBERT CRACKANTHORPE, ALFRED HAYES, MAX BEERBOHM, WILLIAM WATSON, and HENRY JAMES.

The Art Contributions by WALTER CRANE, A. S. HARTRICK, AUBREY BEARDSLEY, ALFRED THORNTON, P. WILSON STEER, JOHN S. SARGENT, A.R.A., SYDNEY ADAMSON, WALTER SICKERT, W. BROWN MACDOUGAL, E. J. SULLIVAN, FRANCIS FORSTER, BERNHARD SICKERT, and AYMER VALLANCE.

A Special Feature of Volume II. is a frank criticism of the Literature and Art of Volume I. by PHILIP GILBERT HAMERTON.

The Yellow Book.

VOL. III. Now ready, pott 4to., 280 pp., 15 Illustrations, with a New Decorative Cloth Cover, price 5s. net.

The Literary Contributions by WILLIAM WATSON, KENNETH GRAHAME, ARTHUR SYMONS, ELLA D'ARCY, JOSÉ MARIA DE HÉRÉDIA, ELLEN M. CLERKE, HENRY HARLAND, •THEO. MARZIALS, ERNEST DOWSON, THEODORE WRATISLAW, ARTHUR MOORE, OLIVE CUSTANCE, LIONEL JOHNSON, ANNIE MACDONELL, C. S., NORA HOPPER, S. CORNISH WATKINS, HUBERT CRACKANTHORPE, MORTON FULLERTON, LEILA MACDONALD, C. W. DALMON, MAX BEERBOHM, and JOHN DAVIDSON.

The Art Contributions by PHILIP BROUGHTON, GEORGE THOMSON, AUBREY BEARDSLEY, ALBERT FOSCHTER, WALTER SICKERT, P. WILSON STEER, WILLIAM HYDE, and MAX BEERBOHM. •

Prospectuses Post Free on Application.

Boston : Copeland & Day.

Hayes, Alfred (1857-1936)
The Vale of Arden. First edition.

www.ingramcontent.com/pod-product-compliance
Lightning Source LLC
Chambersburg PA
CBHW031441280326
41927CB00038B/1486